Whose Shoes?

A Shoe for Every Job

Stephen R. Swinburne

BOYDS MILLS PRESS
HONESDALE, PENNSYLVANIA

Foreword

I've worn lots of different shoes in the many jobs I've had in my life. I found my first job when I was nine years old. I wore old sneakers as a newspaper delivery boy. On Saturday and Sunday mornings, I'd wake early to roll up the newspapers, stuff them in my bicycle basket, and then ride around the neighborhood at breakneck speed. I'd throw the papers at people's houses, hoping not to smash any windows.

I wore grimy sneakers as a dishwasher, new sneakers as a busboy, and black shoes as a waiter. I yanked on hard-toe boots when I drove trucks and laced up high-top sneakers when I made pizzas. I climbed ladders and painted houses in tattered running shoes. I gardened in sandals. Playing drums in a rock band, I wore cool-looking, pointy-tipped black and red slip-ons. When I was a National Park Service ranger, I wore sturdy hiking boots. When I helped sail boats, I wore deck shoes. In the years that I labored in an office, brown wing tips adorned my feet.

Now I write for a living, and I wear whatever I feel like wearing on my feet. Some days I sit at my desk in slippers, and some days I wear wool socks. My feet might have flip-flops on or moccasins or nothing at all. No matter what my feet are wearing, they are always happiest when they are under my desk while I'm writing books.

You, too, might wear many kinds of shoes in your life. Maybe you already know what you want to be. A marine biologist? A professional football player? A teacher? Whatever you do, you'll find the perfect shoe to wear.

Most people wear shoes.

But some people don't.

The first shoes you ever wore were soft and very small.

If it's cold outside,
you wear boots.

If it's hot, you wear flip-flops.

Your favorite shoes might be blue . . .

. . . or silver.

People wear different shoes for different jobs.
Can you tell whose shoes go with what job?

Whose shoes?

A ballerina.

Whose shoes?

A farmer.

Whose shoes?

A fire fighter.

Whose shoes?

An Army
National Guard soldier.

Whose shoes?

A soccer player.

Whose shoes?

A construction worker.

Whose shoes?

A post office worker.

Whose shoes?

A chef.

Whose shoes?

A clown.

Sometimes at the end of the day,
it's hard to get out of your shoes.

But no matter what kind of shoes you wear,
it feels good to take them off.

Whose shoes will you wear one day?

To the new kids in our family—Isabel, Kaito, and Kantaro:
be happy no matter what shoes you wear

My thanks to the following individuals who were photographed for this book:
Hayley Swinburne (ballerina), Jon Wright (farmer), Paul Sherburne (firefighter),
Leslie Butler (Army National Guard soldier), John Oahiambo Aguda (soccer player),
Steve Brown (construction worker), Ann Barnard (post office worker), Serge Roche (chef),
and Robin Zegge (clown). I would also like to thank the kids of Glenwood Elementary
School E-Club, Short Hills, New Jersey; Flood Brook Union School, Londonderry, Vermont;
and Gainfield Elementary School, Southbury, Connecticut.
—S.R.S.

Text and photographs © 2010 by Stephen R. Swinburne

Boyds Mills Press, Inc.
815 Church Street
Honesdale, Pennsylvania 18431
Printed in China

Library of Congress Cataloging-in-Publication Data

Swinburne, Stephen R.
Whose shoes? : a shoe for every job / Stephen R. Swinburne. — 1st ed.
p. cm.
ISBN 978-1-59078-569-0 (hc) • ISBN 978-1-59078-879-0
1. Occupations—Juvenile literature. I. Title.
HF5381.2.S95 2010   331.702—dc22
2009033308

First edition
First Boyds Mills Press paperback edition, 2011
The text of this book is set in 24-point ITC Garamond light.

10 9 8 7 6 5 4 (hc)
10 9 8 7 6 5 4 3 2 1 (pb)